Table Of Contents

Foreword

Is it safe to say that you are troubled 100% of the time with every one of the negative considerations to you? Do you generally imagine that nothing advantageous can happen to you? You won't accomplish what you want? You can't aggregate adequate riches? You can't claim a lavish house?

How frequently do you feel as such?

Achievement relies upon the limits you set to you. Your discernment on the sort of life you need to lead can be incited by your brain. The confidence you have in yourself will lead you to progress. Your conviction, that you can't procure more than whatever you really will put you down. You have set a monetary restriction for yourself.

On the off chance that you are unfaltering that you won't be advanced than you are getting ready for disappointment in profession.
You have made an endless loop to you. You feed your brain with negative contemplations and bomb yourself and this continues to rehash. You have instilled yourself with confined musings and convictions. These limitations and impediments prevent you from carrying on with the ideal life and make you ineffective.

This book will assist you with liberating yourself from your own prohibitive contemplations and urge you to think decidedly. The tips I share here will lead you to progress.

The Millionaire Mindset

Become familiar with The Secrets Of The Most Successful Millionaires And Achieve The Life You Desire Part 1:

Introduction To The Mindset

s

Synopsisynopsis

You might think about what otherworldly powers the rich and well off have? What are their insider facts?

The rich think in an unexpected way. Their tycoon disposition separates them. The needy individuals don't have that sort of mentality that the rich people have.

The Start Point
You can be fruitful in your
monetary and individual life,
through being solid willed. Your
psyche mind is exceptionally
strong and can impact your
cognizant brain. It can either
make you or break you.
For making monetary progress,
you should change your reasoning
example. Also, for that transform
you really want do as follows:
 Begin thinking decidedly. What
you love you start focusing on and
what you focus on you begin
cherishing. So focus on what you
need to be for sure you need. Your
psyche brain will assist you with
accomplishing it.

Make your own way for progress. Attempting to follow others will help you somewhat yet your objective won't be accomplished. You ought to follow your own voice.

On the off chance that you don't cherish yourself you won't ever be rich. Since, in such a case that you don't feel that you merit the best, you can not run after it.

For making progress, you ought to do the very thing you love doing. On the off chance that you are caught in a task, which you disdain, you won't try sincerely as you detest it. Regardless of whether you burn through at least ten hours day by day, you won't succeed.

Quit feeling desirous of fruitful individuals. Desire is a pessimistic inclination and it will just acquire cynicism your life. You will be redirected from the way of accomplishing cash and abundance.

You ought not fault others for your disappointment. Begin assuming liability for whatever occurs in your life. As you might want to assume praise for your prosperity, figure out how to acknowledge your disappointment's too without pointing fingers at others for the equivalent. It will make you a more mindful individual.

Would you like to change your status and need to become rich?

 Get the previously mentioned changes your demeanor towards life. Flourishing and achievement will track down its direction into your existence with your uplifting outlook.Part 2:
Discovering The Purpose Of Your Life

Abstract
Abstract
Without an objective throughout everyday life, you won't know what to do.
It is critical to comprehend the significance of your reality
At the point when you attempt to contemplate what is the mission or reason for your life, you may not get an unmistakable image of it. We need clearness and knowledge for tracking down our genuine reason throughout everyday life.

It is conceivable that you might have numerous objectives in your day to day existence and will most likely be unable to recognize the genuine one, explicit to you. Instructions to bring that one thought out about your psyche that will lead you to progress. What will occur in the event that you can't connect with your fantasies? What is straightaway?

Significant Info

Your association with reality might be the underpinning of your motivation. Not having concluded reason in life doesn't mean you don't have one. It isn't something you will simply awaken to, at some point. You need to strive to decide it. You might not have the choice of picking it

, as you have numerous options. A considerable lot of the decisions may not be veritable.

While focusing on your motivation you should display the capacity to see it. You want make a technique to accomplish your motivation, steps that will lead you to your motivation of life. These strategies and cycles find you the solution for you question and make you say, "This is it!" When you decide your objective, you run after accomplishing it energetically. So the initial step is to go with your ability to understand individuals on a deeper level since it will assist you with recognizing your motivation accurately.

This is the way you go with regards to it:

1. You really want something to record, similar to a piece of paper or word processor in your PC.

2. At the highest point of the page write down, "What is the genuine reason for my life?"3. Anything that answer strikes a chord record it. It very well might be a short expression and not an appropriately outlined sentence as a response.

4. Continue to rehash stage three, until you have composed all that you can imagine on tracking down motivation behind your life.

This is the thing you have been battling to find. Your calling won't make any difference. To some this might seem OK and others might view it as silly. The reason for our life may not be obvious to us due to social preparation.

Your oblivious and cognizant brain will send misleading messages. Be that as it may, whenever you have observed the genuine reason, you feel like it has come from the inward most voice.

Applying rationale and thinking to discover what your perspectives on life are is another technique. The alternate way is to involve rationale and justification behind your circumstance. It will be simple in the event that you are more legitimate in your contemplations.

Apply your absolute educational experience to discover your genuine reason throughout everyday life. Attempt to get where you stand in your current reality.

This is an exceptionally straightforward procedure to follow and henceforth not entirely obvious. What you are doing is, understanding your view on your methodology of life and transforming those into what you see with your own eyes. Where you stand in your current understanding on life, will assist you with finding your objective,
 so you want to discover. Your existence addresses yourself and this assists you with understanding your motivation of life.
The thoughts you have about existence makes up your character, assuming you have a pessimistic mentality towards life that implies you are gloomy individual.

Whenever you are clear with regards to your thoughts, you will observe a reason in life which is attainable and sensible. It resembles a 3D image. At the point when you cut a piece of it, the whole picture is as yet in the more modest piece. You resemble a piece and the entire of the 3D image is reality. You will observe that something is off-base when you have wrong thoughts regarding yourself to you so this strategy will uncover what issues you have and show you reality. These strategies will assist you with discovering your motivation and to know where to go from that point. Assuming that you have a sound viewpoint, you will get results by applying the procedures.

You will discover that the objective and the ability to appreciate people at their core will bring up to your motivation of life in various ways yet they will say exactly the same thing.

Part 3:

Dispose Of Negativity In Your Life

S

Synopsisynopsis

A large portion of us have issues accomplishing what we want. Have we at any point given an idea, concerning why it is unattainable?

Rather than searching for issue inside us, we continue to fault everyone around us for our disappointment. You will fault your country's monetary framework, guardians, kin or even the president yet won't attempt to see what are you lacking?

15

Modifying Your Life

Might there be a basic method for accomplishing what you want, have you at any point mulled over everything? Essential and legitimate response is "The point at which you put stock in something, you get it". This is appropriate for each feature of your life. It incorporates your, relationship, actual prosperity, vocation, etc.

A significant number of us don't understand that, by changing our idea design we roll out sure improvements in our day to day existence. Also, due to this they are dealing with issues all through their life.

A large portion of you see yourself as what others like to make you accept. Assuming that you continue to pay attention to the pessimistic input, you will wind up making an act of allowing individuals to pass judgment on you. You need to pay attention to your inward voice to follow the right way and not everything that others say to you. You are liable for your life and not others. Attempt to get what you truly need and work towards achieving it. Dispose of the multitude of negative musings and get energy your considerations. Make this changing the immediately.

Continuously manifest the best for you as well as your friends and family.

Here is a procedure for you to attempt:

1. Contemplate something/some circumstance in your life that you might want to change immediately. Lead every one of your considerations to the present circumstance.

2. Following the above continue contemplating you and begin having confidence in what you need. Reproduce the subtleties and conditions by shaping a picture of it to you.

3. At the point when you are in a quiet perspective, focus on that change. You ought to do this as frequently as it is feasible for you.

Your oblivious psyche will foster
a propensity for imaging what is
happening which you want.4. With
this positive reasoning, you will
notice the progressions that
happen in your actual world.
When you put positive thinking in
your life, cash, individuals and
considerations, etc will assist you
with arriving at your objective as
though by some sorcery. Positive
change's show their power thusly.
When you begin thinking
decidedly, keep tab of every last
change that is occurring in your
life. Subsequently, you can see, it
is extremely straightforward.
Hence, you have prevented
negative considerations from
entering your psyche. In any case,
this may not be extremely simple
since individuals around you can
acquire the antagonism your life
and in your musings,

this individuals might incorporate your mate, relative, your companion or thereabouts. If conceivable, attempt to get some change them by showing them what changes have positive reasoning has purchased in your life.The most effective way to exploit positive believing is by involving every one of the techniques for driving a delightful and happy

Section 4:

Part 4:

Try not to Restrict Your Mind With Boundaries

S

Synopsisynopsis

Anything that objective you set, you can accomplish it, this you want to continue to remind yourself to be effective.

On the off chance that you have some limited pondering cash you won't ever have the option to aggregate riches.
Here we will attempt to discover, what your confined convictions about cash are, and the way that it is hampering its convergence in your life.

Plan for an impressive future
You will learn about the negative contemplations that don't permit free progression of cash into your life and prevent you from acquiring riches, with assistance of the speculations that I will advance in this book. It you use them in your day to day existence no one can prevent you from being wealthy.

You have solid obstruction towards cash on the off chance that you are not quiet after any of the couple of ideas.

You should wonder why you are not happy doing the ideas, as this will assist you with emerging from the restricted thinking convictions about cash.

While going through the means, you may not be happy with doing some of them. To become familiar with those means continue to rehash them until you foster a solace level. This will assist you with eliminating all the limited reasoning you have about cash. Likewise, you will invite abundance into your life and get out the no cash status in your life. As you go through the means, you will view them as exceptionally basic. In any case, real execution may not be that simple assuming you have solid restricting conviction about cash. Discover the explanations behind such feels and attempt to annihilate them forever from your brain.

You will actually want to check your sentiments, when you attempt to picture what you need throughout everyday life. This will assist you with incorporating it anything that transforms you want to achieve in your life.

For instance, when you are strolling down the road and you see a sumptuous vehicle left external a shop.

You stare at the magnificence of the vehicle. You are gazing at the excellent outside of the vehicle. Indeed, even the select inside of the vehicle is apparent to you.

What musings that are running to you? What are your sentiments at that point? Get to know them as they happen to you so you can record them.

Assuming you are thinking as referenced beneath that implies your comprehension about cash is confined.

1. "The individual driving the vehicle is such a hotshot."

2. "The individual driving the vehicle might have given the cash to the destitute as opposed to spending it on the vehicle."3. "It is out of my spending plan."

4. "A few homes might cost however much this vehicle, so what's the utilization of purchasing such expensive vehicle."

5. "The driver is a consideration searcher, so it isn't something I turn upward to."

-

6. "Individuals, who are incredibly wealthy, will actually want to purchase such a vehicle thus it isn't something I can bear."
7. "It is cool vehicle, however I don't have that sort of cash.
8. "Regardless of whether I work for my entire life I won't make to the point of buying such sumptuous vehicle."
In the event that you have positive pondering cash, you contemplations will be as per the following:

1. "Goodness! This is one of my cherished vehicles."
2. The cash streams into my life with such ease that I need to possibly conclude when I want to buy the vehicle and the vehicle will be mine.
3. "I'm certain this individual can satisfy every one of his desires."
4. "What a sweet vehicle! I realize I will be have one of those later on."
5. "It feels great to realize that individuals can bear the cost of such vehicles."
6. "On the off chance that I let this vehicle come into my life through my positive reasoning, I will have it."
7. "Assuming you tell yourself that you can bear the cost of it". (It may not be imaginable short term but since of positive reasoning you may)

8. "I can as of now feel that the vehicle is a major part of my life." Try to comprehend your inclination, when you get what you want in the wake of thinking emphatically about the circumstance. Your sentiments about cash will be clear when you are on top of the source.

Section 5:
Section 5:
Settle On How Much You Want To Earn
S
Synopsisynopsis
We as a whole long for expanding our pay yet without a legitimate arrangement and its execution, it's unrealistic to accomplish it. In this part I will show you how to show up at your objective and procure more

with the goal that everything you could ever want can work out. Your Income Begin making a picture to you of what you need throughout everyday life. Think exhaustively, what climate you need to be in, what individuals you need to be encircled with. Pick a business, which is practical and will procure you adequate pay. Envision all subtleties minutely. Then, at that point, put forth an objective which is hard to accomplish yet not feasible. At first, consider what you need to accomplish, in one year.

Work out the methodologies for accomplishing your objective for the year. Contemplate every one of the issues you will face and how to handle it. Consider every one of the knocks that you have on your way of accomplishment and learn approaches to staying away from it. Discover what extra preparation or capability you really want for accomplishing your objective. Eliminate every one of the negative musings that enter you mind. Attempt to battle every one of the negative considerations about your pay and business. Continue moving towards your objective by battling with every one of the negative considerations that beat you down.

Record every one of your arrangements you need to reach in one year's time, what steps you will take. Plan each progression and follow them strictly.

Assuming required take direction from the individual whose position you want to be in.

Individuals who are effective,

however not in your line of business will actually want to direct you as well. Have an inspirational perspective and continue to peruse persuasive books for support.

Part 6:
Part 6:
"Fascination" A Powerful Tool
S
Synopsisynopsis
In our everyday discussion, we have all gone over the hypothesis of pattern of energy attracting similar energy with utilization of words like "positive reasoning" thus. The hypothesis might be new for us, however profound scholars have had faith in these speculations for a long time.

Attract It

Our force of reasoning is extremely amazing. It draws in anything we desire into our life. All of the universe will run after accomplishing what we want at whatever point we think or talk about it.

Assuming that we think adversely, we will articulate negative words frequently. "I can not perform" or "I'm not fit for this". The Universe will get these words from your considerations and give it back to you. Antagonism will get you far from your objective.

You can acquire completely changes yourself by being sure about everything in your life. Your life won't change for the time being it will require some investment.

When you seed positive considerations in your day to day existence, it will bear the ideal organic product for you in the long run. Start by having a decent outlook on yourself and love yourself. As you water your seed of positive musings, it changes your life and achieves essential changes. Make certain of what you need throughout everyday life. Whenever you have settled on that, you can request that the universe assist you with accomplishing it. Attempt to make an unmistakable picture of what you want.

Focus on your considerations and watch what you say about your object of want. Act and feel that what you are requesting is coming. You should fool yourself into accepting that what you want is coming and you really want to feel the inclination.

Stand by listening to your nature, co-connect with them and get what the universe is talking about. Get every one of the messages with a receptive outlook. Universe is giving affirmation to you that what you need is coming. You will acquire monetary accomplishment when you are capable relate with the Universe.

Section 7:

Section 7:

Self-Introspection

S

Synopsisynopsis

Wrong ideas to you will lead you no place. You won't ever have the option to achieve the sort of abundance you need.

Many individuals accept that they
don't can bring in the sort of cash
that is required for living
extravagantly. They have
negative thoughts in their psyche.
Others' opinion on them has
turned into the reason for
breaking down their self. They
firmly accept that anyway hard
they work they won't succeed.
These negative musings become
the vision of your life.

Search inside
Try not to have faith in something
since everybody has a similar
thought. Continue to scrutinize
those thoughts. Try not to follow
the group aimlessly. Assuming
enormous quantities of individuals
trust in something that doesn't
really guarantee it to be valid.

 Individuals in the days of yore
accepted that the earth was level
and the sun moved around it.
Today, we as a whole realize this
isn't reality. Despite the fact that
everyone accepted this, that
didn't mean it was correct.
Continually question yourself. It
is simple and enticing to relax
because of these convictions when
we are confronting difficulties
throughout everyday life. These
convictions provide you with a
feeling that everything is good.
You are on the right track to
acknowledge that they can be
bogus.
Assuming you are clear in your
contemplations you will observe
that genuine conviction will
endure for the long haul and some
unacceptable ideas will not. Thus,
eliminate these thoughts from
your life.

Continue to ask yourself, "Would this be able to be relied upon?" What is the assurance that this is reality? "Is this actually reality?" Convictions, which have not been tried, resemble fantasies, they might comfort you at time, you might view them as lovely, think that they are interesting, and as it is what you needed to accept however not really be reality.

Are these your thoughts about cash? Do you make reference to these thoughts regarding cash frequently, truly or nonchalantly? Assuming you do, that implies accidentally these ideas are impacting your relationship with cash.

$ Large numbers of the rich individuals have obtained cash through illicit ways.

$ All the evil on the planet is brought about by cash.

$ I'm not deserving of being rich.
$ Cash is produced by cash. As I don't have cash, I can't become rich.$ Rich individuals are not generally so fair as poor.
$ Whenever it is about cash, certain individuals have all karma.
$ Preposterously rich.
$ Rich individuals are skeptical.
$ I shouldn't be rich and for that reason I am not.
$ Rich individuals are particularly innovative, gifted and wise.
$ Every one of the rich individuals have acquired abundance.

$ Rich individuals are impolite and hostile.
$ All rich individuals are bad. Regardless of whether you will have a wealth of cash or squeeze out a living will rely on your view

of cash. You need to conclude how much cash you need to procure for a sumptuous life and make arrangements likewise.

Do you go through loads of difficulties to bring in cash; would you say you are taking care of your business, which you really disdain? Abundance gets drawn to you effectively or you bring in cash with next to no trouble assuming your thought of abundance is right.

Your vibe great element about cash relies on your thought regarding cash.

In the event that you are alright with in your psyche mind, this is the most extravagant area of feelings. Your past involvement in cash will conclude how agreeable you are with funds.

You can encounter monetary prosperity and create as much abundance as you wish on the off chance that you attempt to eliminate every one of the gloomy sentiments you.

◊ Consider cash energy you move and live with, and that giving this energy access to your life will bring abundance into your life. See what improvement it makes in your day to day existence.
◊ Accept that cash can come to you as effectively as the air you inhale and see what improvement this thought makes in your day to day existence.
You are resolved that having all the abundance you want will make you feel off kilter with the above thought.

Choose to change your ideas about cash, which are negative and are halting the convergence of cash that you are qualified for.
Part
Part 88::
Generosity and Benevolence
Summation
Summation
Consideration is vital, regardless of whether through your actual work or by feelings. It isn't simply valuable to the individual at the less than desirable end yet in addition to yourself. Magnanimity can be displayed through different ways.

The Good
Whenever you focus on others rather than yourself, positive energies develop and circumstances are made for progress. They disentangle

themselves in type of startling and plentiful positive reactions. This might incorporate a difference in conduct from being a misanthrope and mean to benevolence. Best of luck with inflow of bountiful cash might come your direction with such good thoughts.

A parsimonious man chose to pay for the schooling of his companion's child, whose monetary foundation was not all that solid. This signal is out of his personality. Following day out of nowhere he gets installment for the receipt, which has been forthcoming for quite a while.

(In the above situation, the grumpy person comprehended the connection between failing to remember his tackiness and the positive reaction he got from life.

He likewise noticed that the sum, which he liberally gave, was practically equivalent to the sum he got from the surprising installments)
Kindheartedness and liberality
You can acquire best of luck your life by being benevolent and liberal towards others. At the point when an individual sends appreciation and generosity to his companions and various clients he was showered with uplifting news as cash, deals and other best of luck.

Have generosity at work.
To draw in cash you really want to have generosity towards the others around you as well as situation and circumstance around you. Generosity in your work will draw in heaps of cash into your life.

Out progression of surplus generosity will make inflow of surplus cash. For instance assuming a sales rep invests his 100 percent energy in his work, it is conceivable that he will encounter best of luck as more interest, more work and more open doors and so on

This model shows you that the utilization of altruism can be straightforwardly connected with cash and achievement.

For what reason do generosity and kindheartedness draw in cash? Consider cash a power and not a thing. The power has confidence in empowering common benefits and connection between people. Cash is the power for human exchange and correspondence.

Cash can measure up to language. Language empowers people to cooperate with different people.

Consider an individual who chooses to stay quiet and needs to hush up about every one of the words.

Will this choice assistance him? Most certainly no! Language itself is for correspondence. Language develops and is helpful provided that we use it for

correspondence. The more you use it the more you get it and can connect with it. Language empowers a solitary individual to speak with the entire society. We don't store language. Thusly we can presume that the more individuals that utilization our language, the simpler it is to relate with others. This can be applied to cash.

Cash is like language. At the point when we relate through cash with others, cash develops.

At the point when we help other people to flourish and attempt to support accomplishment in people around us, we will draw in cash. Altruism and kindness will draw in more cash into our life. The more you give, the more you get.Part 9:: Trust That It Is Easy To Make Money

Synopsi

Synopsiss

We have a few time or the other heard that we could accomplish what we genuinely have confidence in. Having confidence in something will assist you with accomplishing it.

Many individuals will dispose of this hypothesis, while some might have taken a stab at making it happen yet might not have really done as such and still other people who have attempted it and have tasted accomplishment through it.

Be that as it may, acquiring achievement is exceptionally difficult, as you need to follow the means in this trusting system and use it in support of yourself.
Trust It
Answer a couple of the inquiries:
◊ Do you accept with all confidence that there are different ways of arriving at your objective and you simply need to track down them?
◊ Do you have complete confidence in yourself and your capacity to accomplish anything that you want monetarily and actually?
◊ Do you totally accept that you will be shown the correct course at right time and regardless of where you are presently, you will arrive at your objective?

In the event that your solution for large numbers of the above questions is in bad, it won't lead you to where you wish to go.
You want to totally accept that all that will help you out. The conviction that you can observe a solution for each question that emerges while knowing and accepting that you can and you will.
Instructions to acquire such an undeniable degree of self-assurance

Start with little advances. Start
by focusing on little issues in your
day to day existence like, in the
event that you can't observe the
keys, continue to let yourself
know that you will track down
them.
Whenever you truly observe them,
you will begin putting stock in this
interaction. While doing an
undertaking with a severe cutoff
time continue to guarantee
yourself

that you will complete your task
inside the cutoff time and when
you have completed the
undertaking you have created
trust in yourself. By acquiring this
change yourself, you will figure
out how to be certain with regards
to yourself.

Quit stressing, on the grounds
that stressing resembles not
confiding in yourself. Sentences
like, "I stress since I may not be
capable completion the tests",
show your absence of certainty.
By stressing, you can't change
what is going on.
As you begin accepting yourself in
settling on little choices, it will
end up being a propensity with
you. In this manner, when you
deal with more serious issues
throughout everyday life, you
know what to do. You have quit
stressing and are confronting
difficulties with loads of
fearlessness. You know what to do
and can accomplish what you wish
for.

Ventures for knowing all about self-conviction a training may yet you will invest in some opportunity to accomplish this propensity.

 Monetary achievement relies exceptionally upon self-conviction. Without this, nothing will seem OK.Wrapping Up Everyone needs to be rich. Some of them have effectively accomplished this and some are attempting to accomplish. Numerous ways will lead you to monetary achievement and the importance for abundance is different for every one of us. Regardless of how you characterize abundance, your thought of abundance will assist you with making monetary progress.

Having right demeanor towards
cash assists you with achieving
monetary achievement. It has its
own quality, personality and
power.
Seeing how changing your idea
about cash in your circumstance is
vital.

www.ingramcontent.com/pod-product-compliance
Lightning Source LLC
Chambersburg PA
CBHW051403150726
48000CB00003B/1313